SELF-PUBLISHING YOUR BOOK IN MULTIPLE FORMATS

How to Set Up Your Book in Print, E-Book, Audiobook, Video, Online Course, and PDF Formats

by Gini Graham Scott, Ph.D.

Author of 150+ Books
100 from Changemakers Publishing

SELF-PUBLISHING YOUR BOOK IN MULTIPLE FORMATS

Copyright © 2017 by Gini Graham Scott

All rights reserved. No part of this book may be used or reproduced by any means, graphic, electronic, or mechanical, including photocopying, recording, taping or by any information storage retrieval system without the written permission of the author except in the case of brief quotations embodied in critical articles and reviews.

TABLE OF CONTENTS

INTRODUCTION 5
CHAPTER 1: PREPARING YOUR MANUSCRIPT FOR PUBLICATION 7
   Writing and Preparing Your Book for Publication 8
   Recording, Transcribing, and Editing Your Book 9
   Preparing Your Files for Publication 10
CHAPTER 2: DECIDING HOW TO PUBLISH YOUR BOOK. 13
   Saying No to Traditional Publishing 14
   Using Self-Publishing to Build Your Platform to Get a Traditional Publishing Deal 16
   Deciding on How to Publish a Longer Book - One Book or More 17
CHAPTER 3: DECIDING ON THE FORMAT FOR YOUR BOOK 19
   Deciding on the Format - Print or E-Book 19
   Publishing a Print Book 20
      Hardcover versus Paperback 20
      What Size to Choose 21
      Print-on-Demand Versus Printing a Run of Books 21
CHAPTER 4: CHOOSING A PRINT-ON-DEMAND PLATFORM 23
   Deciding What Platforms to Use 24
      Why Publish on CreateSpace 25
      Why Publish on IngramSpark -- and Some Challenges to Using this Platform 26
      Publishing an E-Book 28
   A Recommended Order for Publishing Your Books 29
   Getting an ISBN 30
   Selling Your Book 30
CHAPTER 5: DECIDING TO CREATE AN AUDIOBOOK 33
   Why Are Audiobooks Growing So Rapidly 34
   Creating an Audiobook 34
   Hiring a Narrator 35

CHAPTER 6: HIRING A NARRATOR THROUGH THE ACX PLATFORM 37
  Setting Up Your Book to Find a Narrator 38
  From a Narrator Accepting Your Offer to a Completed Audiobook 39
CHAPTER 7: THE BASICS OF CREATING YOUR BOOK AS A COURSE 43
  What Makes a Good Course 44
  Creating Your Course 45
CHAPTER 8: ORGANZING YOUR COURSE AND CREATING YOUR VIDEOS AND OTHER MATERIALS 47
  Organizing Your Course 47
  Creating Videos for Your Course 49
  Pricing Your Course 51
CHAPTER 9: CREATING YOUR BOOK OR CHAPTERS AS A PDF 53
  Creating Your PDF 54
  Creating a Cover for Your PDF 55
  Including Sales Material in Your Book 56
  Selling Your Book through Your Website, Landing Page, or Online Marketing 56
  Turning Your PDF into a Published Book 57
ABOUT THE AUTHOR 59

INTRODUCTION

Today, a book can be published in multiple formats. Traditionally, books have been in print as hardbacks and paperbacks.

But between 1998 and 2003, the first e-books struggled onto the market and Sony introduced the Librié, the first e-book reader with electronic ink technology. Then, in 2007, everything changed with the introduction of the Kindle by Amazon, which was the real dawn of the e-book, just a decade ago.

Around this time, in about 2008, the new print-on-demand technology opened up new opportunities for publishing short runs of books, rather than depending on a printing press for a minimum run of several hundred books or more. The beginnings of the rapid growth of the self-publishing industry dates back to then. And in the last five years, the industry has grown even more rapidly to over a million books published a year.

Meanwhile, many new formats have emerged for books. Ironically, audiobooks have had a long history, dating back the beginnings of the phonograph by Thomas Edison in 1877. As a result of this new invention, many short, spoken word recordings were sold on cylinder in the late 1800s and early 1900s. However, these round cylinders were limited to about four minutes each, so it was impractical to publish a book. Later flat platters made it possible to record up to 12 minutes, but this was still impractical for longer works. So for a while, audiobooks were created mainly for the blind and for poetry, plays, and other short works.

Then, in the 1970s, the cassette tape gained popularity. Though it was invented in 1963 and a few libraries began distributing books on tape, the invention of the Walkman and other cheap players led to the beginnings of the commercial market, which really took off in 1986. The market grew even more with the introduction and growing popularity of the CD in 2003 through 2008. After that, digital downloads became increasingly popular, and more recently smart phones and tablets have provided another platform, so now audiobooks are available in multiple formats, including cassette tapes, CDs, **MP3, and** downloadable digital formats. Audible, purchased by Amazon in 2008, has become the largest audiobooks distributor.

Plus now books have been turned into videos and online courses, while chapters have been turned into articles and blogs that are used as promotional introductions to the full book, while blogs and articles are often combined into books.

Self-Publishing Your Book in Multiple Formats is designed to help writers take advantage of the many formats for publishing and selling books. It features an introduction to the different platforms and how to prepare and publish your manuscript in each format. By doing so, you can take advantage of the multiple approaches for selling your book to customers who like to read books in different ways.

To this end, the book features the following topics:
- preparing your manuscript for publication,
- deciding how to publish your book,
- deciding on the format for your book,
- choosing a print-on demand platform,
- creating an audiobook,
- hiring a narrator for your audiobook,
- creating your book as an online course,
- organizing your course and creating videos and other materials,
- creating your book or chapters as a PDF.

Future books in the series will deal with how to build an audience and market and promote your book in different formats.

CHAPTER 1: PREPARING YOUR MANUSCRIPT FOR PUBLICATION

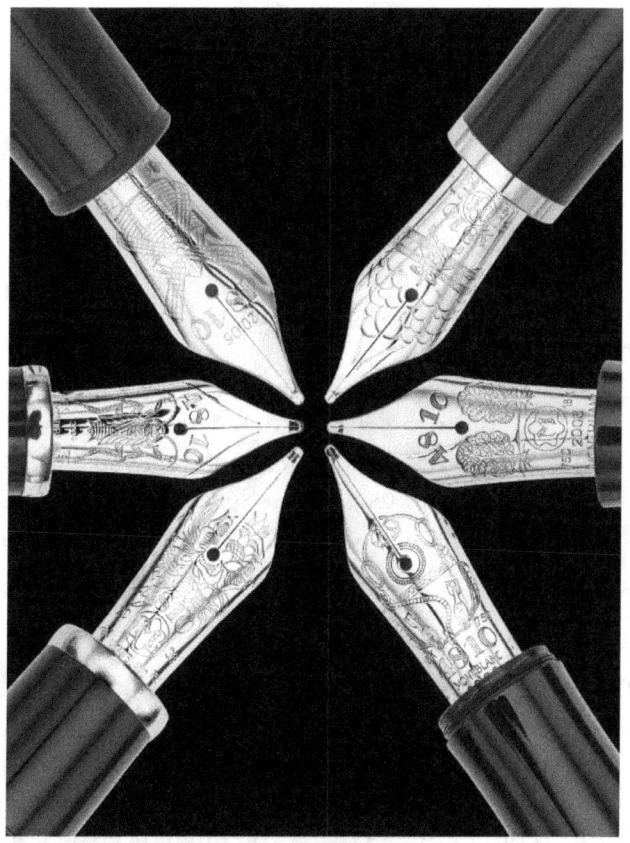

 A question that many authors ask me is "How should I self-publish my book?"
 Some have been introduced to self-publishing by workshops, seminars, and online pitches that offer them an opportunity to write, publish, and distribute their book for anywhere from about $1500 to $35,000. The less expensive offers are essentially from printers who set up your ready-to print book for distribution on Amazon or Ingram, plus they might feature your

book in an online catalog of their books; Some add a few thousand if you need help in getting your book ready for print. The more expensive programs of $15,000 and up generally help you get your book written by advising you on how to outline it, write or record and transcribe chapters, and then edit the manuscript into your final book. Then they print and help with marketing.

There are also hybrid publishing programs, some offshoots of established companies costing about $7,000 to $15,000, with mixed results. Sometimes these hybrids help an author publish and promote their book effectively, though the writer has to make a big investment. In other cases, authors complain the company did little for them, apart from printing their book, and they feel ripped off by the unfulfilled promises to do extensive marketing and promotion.

But the process doesn't have to be that complicated and expensive. In the following chapter, I'll describe the basics of preparing your manuscript for publication. In a subsequent chapter I'll cover what platform to use: CreateSpace, IngramSpark, or both. I'll also discuss how to create your cover for different platforms and how to set up your book to become an e-book, audiobook, and online course.

Writing and Preparing Your Book for Publication

Once you have a general idea of what your book is about, you can outline it into chapters and subsections of a chapter, and then write or record those. Perhaps you might need an hour or two of assistance to guide you, but it seems like these expensive programs make the steps more involved than they need to be. As long as you work at your own pace and set aside some time to write, you can get it done.

Another good approach is to divide your book into smaller books, so you get something published, and later combine these together into a longer book. Once you have about 50-75 pages, that's enough for a mini-book, and some people do even shorter books of 25-50 pages. This mini-book approach works well for how-to, self-help, and popular business books, where you give out tips on how to do something, and you plan to use the book to increase your credibility, visibility, authority, and branding to get more customers or clients or set up speaking engagements. But if you want your book to appeal to bookstores and libraries, your book should usually be about 150 pages or more.

Recording, Transcribing, and Editing Your Book

If you record your book, you can talk into your phone or other recording device, do an interview, or record a workshop or seminar. Afterwards, however you do it, get it transcribed. Then, figure on editing the manuscript yourself or hire an editor, since you can't normally go directly from a transcript to a finished book. There are some software programs to automatically turn your recording into text, such as Dragon software, but automated transcribing generally only works if you have a single clear voice. Otherwise, if you have a workshop with multiple voices or record in a noisy environment, the software can get confused, and you can end up with gibberish featuring short phrases, skips, and other mishaps, as I discovered in sending some workshop files to a couple of automated online voice-to-text services. So where you have multiple voices that sometimes talk over each other, you need a human transcriber, typically at $1 a minute from a service like Rev.com or a local transcriber.

Once you have the transcript, figure on about an hour for editing and rewriting for every 750-1000 words. Plus you may want to add other ideas suggested by the topics you cover briefly in your recording -- and some editors knowledgeable about your subject can add material for you if you don't do this yourself. Aside from top of your head additions, Internet research is another source of additional material.

Preparing Your Files for Publication

Once you have written and edited your book, you are almost ready to publish it. You then have to format your copy and any photos or illustrations, depending on the platform you choose for publication.

If you have illustrations or photos, insert them where you want them in the book. Just click insert picture in your document and add the file. Ideally, you should take, scan, or purchase photos so they are 300 dpi (dots per inch) or higher resolution. You can get away with lower resolution photos in your book's interior on most publishing platforms, though the images can appear fuzzy due to the lower resolution. But if they are small interior photos or illustrations, they will probably look okay.

You also need to format your book according to the finished size you want. Most trade books are now 6"x9", so it's usually a good idea to choose that format, though if you want to show off photos and illustrations in your book, such as a gift or children's book, a 7"x10" or 8"x10" is a good size. For workbooks and handbooks, an 8 1/2"x11" format is ideal, and if you want a small pocket-sized book, some writers like a 5 ½" x 8 ½" book.

Whatever size you choose, set up your margins based on the number of pages. Typically I use .75" on the left and right and 1" on the top and bottom for a book of 350 pages or less. If the book has more pages, allow a larger margin on the right and left, say 1".

Also, choose your font and font size based on your type of book. A common font type is Times New Roman, though some other fonts are recommended, such as Bookman or Garamond. I usually use 12-point type for books with a lot of text; 13-point if I want a slightly larger book with less text, and 14-point for gift and children's books.

Use the headers in Word to mark each chapter and subsection, and Word will create your Table of Contents. Adjust your copy so any chapters and section headers, such as for a

Preface, Foreword, Acknowledgments, Author's Bio, and Contact Information, start on the right or odd number page. That way, when the reader opens your book, each chapter or section header will pop out on the right.

Finally, once your book is edited, formatted, and ready to go in a Word document, you can use that to create your e-book. For a print book, it is preferable and sometimes mandatory to turn your document into a PDF with embedded fonts. An embedded font is one which will always appear the same way as it does in your PDF file, so no matter what fonts a reader has on their computer, they will see the same font style you chose. One way to embed your fonts is to print your Word document as an Adobe PDF (don't just save it as a regular PDF), and instead of printing a standard PDF, set your printer for Adobe, click properties, and turn your Word doc into a PDF/X1-a:2001 document. Then, print. That will embed any fonts. If you use any special fonts and get a notice that the program can't embed these fonts, usually because you don't have a special license for them, choose another font -- preferably a common one -- and try again.

You can use your original Word document if you use CreateSpace as your publishing platform, but it is preferable to use a printed PDF. But if you publish on IngramSpark, you need a PDF with embedded fonts, such as a PDF/X1-a:2001 document.

Now you've got the interior of your book ready to publish. I'll cover how to prepare your cover in a subsequent chapter.

CHAPTER 2: DECIDING HOW TO PUBLISH YOUR BOOK

Once a manuscript is completed, usually as a Word document or PDF or both, the next question is "What publishing platform should I choose?"

Many writers dream of traditional publishing. They envision a big enough advance to give them at least a small monthly stipend while they write their book. They imagine the prestige and sense of "you made it," that comes with a traditional publishing deal with a well-recognized publisher.

But for most writers, traditional publishing is not a realistic option. It is unlikely to get a publishing deal as a relatively unknown writer. It takes a long time to get published. Advances from small publishers, if you get an offer, are miniscule. Publishers do little to market and promote you unless you are already famous. And you may be expected to contribute towards your book's publication by many publishers.

So that leaves the various self-publishing platforms -- primarily CreateSpace or IngramSpark for print books; Kindle or IngramSpark for e-books; and ACX or other audio producers for audiobooks. Or call publishing your own book "independent publishing," where you create an identity as a small publisher -- and you publish your book yourself.

To help you decide what to do, here's a more detailed look at the various publishing options.

Saying No to Traditional Publishing

Sometimes writers still hold out a hope of traditional publishing. But this is unrealistic for most writers for several reasons:

- Traditional publishers and agents typically want an author who already is famous or has a large following as a speaker or through a social media platform. So unless you have a great novel that is so powerful and unique that it speaks for itself, you are unlikely to get a publishing deal with any major publisher or publishing imprint. This is especially true if you are writing in the more popular and competitive genres today -- self-help, popular business, health and fitness, and memoirs.

- You might still get an offer from a smaller publisher, but you are likely to get a very small advance -- about $1000-2000. Or you may be offered a co-publishing or hybrid publishing deal, which can work if you can come up with $5000-10,000, sometimes more. Then, the publisher can help by marketing your book through its distribution network, sending information about your book to trade publications and reviewers, and including your book in its catalog. But often small or hybrid publishers don't do much additional marketing and publicity. And some have gotten many complaints from writers who felt they spent a lot of money on publishing and marketing deals, but sold few books. Thus, sales are likely to be small, unless you do a lot of the publicity yourself or pay the publisher a large amount of money to do it for you, with mixed results.

    - Your book won't come out for a year or two -- commonly in about 18 months. So if you want a book to build your credibility and help you get speaking engagements or more customers or clients, you won't have your book to help you now.

    - If you later become unhappy that the publisher isn't doing enough for you, you will be locked into an agreement for that book, and you may have to pay the publisher to get out of it, or write another book. For example, one writer complained about spending $15,000 with one publisher but got few sales, and it cost him another $750 to get out of his exclusive contract.

    - Unless you have written or revised the contract to permit you to have control over audio rights or dramatic rights, you won't be able to turn your book into an audiobook, develop videos for courses based on your book, or negotiate the rights to a film based on your book.

    - The publisher will have control over your book, which can be fine if you have a major publisher that will back up your book with a big publicity and marketing campaign. But with a smaller publisher, you still have to give up control, which might become a problem if you disagree with some of the publishing decisions, such as for the cover, title, and positioning. You might have the right to provide some input, but after that, the publisher has the right to decide what to do, even if you have gotten no or very little advance.

    - You commonly have to write a longer book, such as for 250-350 pages, and you may not have the time, interest, or information to write that much. But traditional publishers generally don't want smaller books, since they can't charge enough for them to make a sufficient profit. And smaller books don't have the gravitas of the longer books.

Using Self-Publishing to Build Your Platform to Get a Traditional Publishing Deal

Thus, given the possible problems with traditional publishing, many writers self-publish -- or independently publish -- a shorter book now -- say 50-150 pages. Then, they use that to build their platform -- essentially by increasing their following and media presence, so after a year or two of platform building, they can go to a traditional publisher or agent, who may feel they finally have enough of a platform to take a chance on their book.

But if you do seek out a traditional publisher at this stage, the key to success is not to pitch your original book, unless you have a large sales track record, say at least 5000 or more sales in a year. Otherwise, if you have only a small number of sales, most publishers and agents will consider that book dead in the water. Instead, you can pursue one of these two strategies, which I and many authors have done successfully.

1) Pitch what you have already written as a small section of the larger manuscript, and point out in your proposal that you have used this mini-book to help you build your audience through speaking, the social media, and other methods. For example, I did this in selling *The Battle Against Internet Book Piracy* to Allworth Press, which published it as *Internet Book Piracy*.

2) Pitch your complete manuscript as a new manuscript, which is a follow-up or sequel to what you previously wrote. In this case, you revise what you previously wrote, so this becomes an updated section of the new manuscript. Then, as above, explain that you have written this first book to build your platform. For example, I sold *Lies and Liars: Why and How Sociopaths Lie and How to Detect and Deal with Them* to Skyhorse Publishing, based on using this approach, after I had written *The Truth About Lying*.

If you still are set on finding a traditional publisher, even after publishing a book, you need a proposal for a non-fiction book. This proposal consists of about 15 pages, with an overview and sections on the appeal of the book, the market and competition, your past publicity and media presence, your plans to promote the book, your author's bio, and a chapter by chapter outline, plus an introduction and chapter or two of your proposed book. Figure on about 25-40 more pages for your sample chapters, or about 35 to 50 pages for the whole proposal. For a novel, you need a synopsis and the completed manuscript.

Deciding on How to Publish a Longer Book - One Book or More

If you have a completed manuscript ready to go, decide whether to publish it as a single book, if it is over 150 pages, or break it into smaller books.

If it makes sense, you can divide a longer book into two or three shorter books and publish these separately, rather than combining those parts into the complete book. This divide and conquer approach works well for a self-help or how-to business book, where each part of the larger book becomes a stand-alone book. I've done this with several books, such has *The Complete Guide to Email Marketing, Make More Money with Your Book, Make More Money with Your Product or Service,* and *What's Your Dog Type?* One approach is to give each smaller book the full title plus a subtitle that begins Part I, Part II, and so forth. Another approach, which I have also used, is to come up with titles for the smaller books. For instance, *What's Your Dog Type?* was divided into *Discovering Your Dog Type, Getting Help from Your Dogs, Getting Even More Help from Your Dogs,* and *Using the Dog Type System in Your Everyday Life.*

If you create a series of smaller books, you can publish them as you complete them or publish all of the books at the same time. Once all of the smaller books are complete, you can publish all the parts together as a single book – which is a bargain for a reader who wants to get all of the parts, since the cost is about $20 to $25 for a 350 page book instead of about $10 a book for each of the parts. But if someone just wants to read one section, the just buying a smaller book makes sense.

So now you are ready to publish and ready to decide which of the self-publishing platforms are best for you. I'll describe what to do in the next chapter.

CHAPTER 3: DECIDING ON THE FORMAT FOR YOUR BOOK

Once your manuscript is ready as a Word document, the next step is deciding on the format for your book - hardcover, paperback, or e-book.

Deciding on the Format - Print or E-Book

Sometimes writers decide to only publish an e-book, which is fine, though you are missing out on the market for people who like a physical book, and you will have more opportunities for reviews if you publish in both print and e-book formats.

Another reason to publish both a print and an e-book is you already have the necessary interior and the front cover already completed. All you additionally need to do is to set up a back cover and, if the book is large enough, the title and author copy for the spine. This back cover can be relatively easy to set up if you include two or three main elements -- a block of text for your copy, which includes the book description, and optionally, an author's bio, and your photo if you want to include that. Normally, the publisher will add the ISBN number in a box set aside for that on the back cover, so you don't have to add that.

Publishing a Print Book

When you publish a print book, the most common format is a paperback, which you can publish on both CreateSpace and IngramSpark as print on -demand books, as well as through independent printers and publishing companies. But if you want a hardcover book, you have to publish with IngramSpark or an independent printer/publishing company. You can use the same interior with both hardcover and paperback books, though your cover setup will differ slightly, since you have to allow for some extra space on the edges for the hardback cover binding.

Hardcover versus Paperback

In deciding on whether to publish in hardcover, paperback, or both, take into consideration the cost for both retail and your own purchase price. A hardcover is good for certain types of books, such as children's picture books, library books, and gift-books, because they will get a lot of wear -- as do picture books and library books, or because they look more elegant when you show them off or give them as presents. Otherwise, paperbacks are more common, since they sell for less, and if you are going to buy your own books, hardbacks cost more because they are more expensive to print.

Generally, it will cost about $2-3 more to buy an author's copy of your hardcover book, and when you add in the mark-up for the distributor and retailer, that translates into charging at least $10 more for a hardback copy at retail, though $15 to $20 more is common for retail pricing. For instance, a paperback that retails for $14.95 will often cost $24.95 to $29.95 if it's a hardback. So consumers more typically will opt to buy the paperback, so you'll sell more of those.

What Size to Choose

As for size, the most popular format is a 6"x9" book, though you can select other sizes. The other most common sizes include a 5 ½"x8 ½", 7"x10", 8"x10", or 8 ½"x11 ½" size. The smaller 5 ½"x8 ½" format might be a good choice, if you have a small number of pages and want a book that's easy to carry around, such as in a pocket or purse. A 7"x10" or 8"x10" format is good if your book has illustrations and charts, so they show up better. The 8 ½" x 11 ½" size is good for workbooks, manuals, and instructional materials, or if you want to turn a regular sized PDF into a book. You can choose any number of custom sizes, though the sizes available are more limited when you select a template, such as when using CreateSpace.

Print-on-Demand Versus Printing a Run of Books

Sometimes the question comes up as to whether to select a print-on-demand publisher, such as the two most popular ones -- CreateSpace and IngramSpark, or opt for a short run with a regular printer/publisher. Today, most self-publishers choose the print-on-demand (POD) option, because it is less expensive and therefore less risky, since you aren't paying several hundred or thousand dollars to print up at least 100 to 500 books for a typical initial run. The cost per book is a little more for a POD than the cost of a book in a print-run book, because you are printing fewer books at a time and POD pricing is based on printing individual books. The advantage with a print-on-demand publisher is that once you set up your master for publication, you can print any number of copies --

even no copies, if you just want to post your book and wait for sales.

But, while the cost per copy may generally be somewhat less for print-run than print-on-demand books, you have to figure on the cost of the minimum number of copies you have to buy and determine if you have a way to sell them. If not, the safer approach is to use POD publishing in the beginning before you build up a large number of sales. And that's what most self-publishers do now. They select a print-on-demand arrangement and order however many books they want to sell -- or minimally they purchase one or two display copies to use in taking orders from customers.

CHAPTER 4: CHOOSING A PRINT-ON-DEMAND PLATFORM

Unless you are using a book packager or hybrid publisher, the major options for self-publishing are CreateSpace and IngramSpark for print and Kindle and an IngramSpark for e-books. Plus a few other companies are involved in e-book distribution, most notably Smashwords and Draft2Digital.

How do you decide what to do -- use some of the platforms or all of them? And what are the major considerations to help you decide? Here I'll discuss the different options.

Deciding What Platforms to Use

Which platform should you choose? Should you publish a print book on CreateSpace and an e-book through Kindle, publish through IngramSpark or IngramSpark's e-book platform, or choose different print and e-book companies? While you can publish the print and e-book separately, say by publishing a print book through CreateSpace and an e-book through IngramSpark, more generally, you'll publish a print and e-book with the same publishing family -- CreateSpace and Kindle, or IngramSpark and its epub. Plus other e-book options include Smashwords and Draft2Digital, and you can publish directly on some of the e-book platforms, such as Nook, Kobo, Barnes and Noble, and iTunes.

My recommendation, which is what most independent publishers do, is to publish on all of the platforms, and use Smashwords and Draft2Digital as intermediaries to publish on the other major e-book platforms. Otherwise, you have to set up each of these accounts separately, and sometimes, if you only have one or a small number of books, you may not be approved for that platform. However, there are some good reasons to publish on CreateSpace only, which I'll explain.

To publish on both CreateSpace and IngramSpark, you need to leave unchecked the extended distribution options for libraries and bookstores on CreateSpace. To publish on both Kindle and IngramSpark's e-book platforms, you can't participate in KDP Select. When you do sign-up for KDP Select, you give Kindle an exclusive e-book publishing option for 90 days, which is renewed for an additional 90 days at the end of each option period unless you opt out of a future renewal. However, you can participate in KDP Select for the first 90 days and not renew, and then participate in other e-book platforms. Deciding what to do is a marketing question for a later discussion of marketing strategies.

Following are the basic benefits of choosing different platforms.

Why Publish on CreateSpace

CreateSpace is the easiest POD platform to publish on. It is especially designed for new authors and independent publishers who only want to publish a paperback. You can obtain a free ISBN, which is fine if you don't care about bookstore or library sales, since it will identify CreateSpace as the publisher wherever that ISBN is used (such as on Amazon), although you can still put your own publishing logo on the book. Alternatively, you can get an ISBN for $99 from CreateSpace or bring your own ISBN from Bowker, and then you will be recognized as the publisher.

Another advantage of CreateSpace is that you can choose from 30 different templates, where you can select various style, type, and color options. In most cases, you select a photo to fit a designated space in the template's front cover, though some templates are designed for type only. A few offer the option of uploading a completed front cover, uploading the front and back cover separately, or uploading a complete cover. Or you can submit a PDF with the cover completed according to the book's specs, based on the size and number of pages.

The cost of buying your own books from CreateSpace is also less than publishing on IngramSpark. Generally, your copies cost about $1.50 less per copy, so you can set a lower retail, which might boost sales (though if you publish on both platforms, set the same retail price for both).

Another advantage of publishing on CreateSpace is the publishing process is faster. Generally, it takes one day to get an approval if you have met all of the publishing requirements, versus two to three days with IngramSpark.

A big reason to publish only on CreateSpace is if you are mainly publishing your book to promote your business or sell copies at the back of the room at presentations and workshops. In this case, you don't care about bookstore or library sales. Rather, you hope to keep the cost as low as possible for book giveaways or your own retail sales. Since the quality is about the same whether you publish with CreateSpace or IngramSpark, the cost savings is a good reason for choosing this option. For example, say a small book through CreateSpace will cost $2.15 plus shipping, while the same small book published by IngramSpark will be about $3.60 plus shipping. If you order 100 books, you are saving about $150 on a CreateSpace book.

The ease of preparing your manuscript is another benefit. Essentially all you need to publish on CreateSpace is a completed Word or PDF document in the size of the book you want to publish (ie: 6"x9," 8"x10," or "8 ½" x 11") with the appropriate margins based on the number of pages (ie: .75" if under 399 pages; 1" if 400 pages or more). Additionally, you only need your back cover copy, title, sub title if any, description, and a photo if required by the template, plus some information to set up your account, describe your book in more detail, and choose five keywords. Once you know what you are doing, it will take about 2-3 hours to provide the needed information and submit your book.

Why Publish on IngramSpark -- and Some Challenges to Using this Platform

The key reason for publishing with IngramSpark is that this will open up library and bookstore sales that are generally not available for CreateSpace books -- largely because CreateSpace only offers a 25% discount on retail purchases and no returns. By contrast, IngramSpark offers a standard 55% discount for wholesalers and large quantity sales and 40% for smaller retail orders. Also, book reviewers and the media are more likely to take a book published and distributed through IngramSpark more seriously; so if your book might appeal to a broad audience, that's another good reason to publish through IngramSpark. Then, too, you can publish a hardcover edition with IngramSpark, and many libraries and book stores prefer to buy hardbacks, whereas CreateSpace only publishes paperbacks.

On the downside, it's more expensive to publish a paperback on IngramSpark, though there are substantial savings if you are a member of the Independent Book Publishers Association (IBPA), which costs about $129 a year. The basic expenses waived for IBPA members are the initial $49 account set-up fee, as well as the $25 set-up fee and $25 market access fee for each book. Plus, there's a discount on buying an ISBN for each book from Bowker. Normally, it costs $125 for one ISBN, 10 for $295, or 100 for $575, though the IBPA member discount is about 15%.

Another potential difficulty in publishing through IngramSpark is that the company is more particular about how you submit your book interior and cover. You have to first obtain your ISBN with information about your book, usually from Bowker, though you can buy an ISBN from IngramSpark for about $85. In addition, you have to have a 300 dpi PDF in which all of the fonts are embedded, and ideally all of the photos in the PDF meet that 300 dpi standard, although lower resolution photos can still be published.

The cover standards are even more exacting. The cover has to meet certain design specs, although you can generate a template for formatting your cover based on the size of your book, the number of pages, and whether it is a paperback or hardback. Then, you have to follow that template exactly, so your design fits within the parameters provided, and no text or images can overlap into a pink border area. Otherwise, your design will be rejected, and you have to submit it again. So unless you are a graphic designer, you may need to hire a book cover designer to create the cover for you -- which can range from about $300-1500, depending on the type of cover you want and the cost of creating the cover from scratch. But one way to get the cost down is to first create your cover in CreateSpace using one of its templates. Then, a graphic designer can work from that design for much less, say about $50-$100.

If you can overcome all these hurdles, and you want your book in bookstores and libraries and want to increase your chances of getting reviews, definitely publish your book on IngramSpark, and additionally publish on CreateSpace.

Publishing an E-Book

Increasingly, some writers are only publishing e-books, and that can be an easier, faster way to go, although you are cutting out a large percentage of readers who still like a physical book. In fact, according to the *Publishers Weekly* for September 25, 2017, e-book sales have leveled off, while print books are increasing again. So I don't recommend only publishing an e-book, though you can do it.

Kindle, like CreateSpace, makes publishing an e-book very easy. After setting up your account, you only need to have a Word file, which is preferred to a PDF. However, if you publish on CreateSpace first, Kindle can convert your PDF proof into a Kindle document, though you get a caution that's it's better to upload your original Word file.

Then, you only need a front cover image of your book. If you have already published your book through CreateSpace, you can use the front cover created there. Otherwise, create a front cover using the same format you might use for a print book cover. For example, a 6"x9" format is fine, and you can create it yourself or work with a book designer. Kindle will assign you an ISBN if you don't have one.

To publish an e-book with IngramSpark or on other e-book platforms, you need an interior and cover in an epub format. Plus you need an ISBN for an e-book. You can use various services to create this epub file for you, or you can create it yourself using e-book creation software, such as Calibre, which you can download for free. Converting a Word to an epub file will usually work, although there can be some glitches, which professionals who do e-book conversions will know about. For instance, you can't break up series of numbers with headers; instead you have to turn the numbers into bullet points for Calibre to read and convert the files.

A Recommended Order for Publishing Your Books

Given the way these different publishing platforms work, I recommend the following order.

1. Publish on CreateSpace. This way you can easily design your cover using one of the templates, and that can help you set up your cover for Kindle. The template can also be a guide for setting up your IngramSpark cover. You can use all of the back cover text and descriptive information you write for CreateSpace for IngramSpark, too.

2. Publish on Kindle. You can take the original document prepared for your CreateSpace interior and use that on Kindle, or use the PDF created through CreateSpace. Plus CreateSpace will generate the cover you need to publish on Kindle. You just have to add some account information, details about pricing and distribution, and two extra keywords, and you are done.

3. Publish on IngramSpark as a hardcover or paperback, using the appropriate ISBN, which you have purchased from Bowker or can purchase through IngramSpark. Start with your original Word document and use it to create a PDF designed for printing. Instead of saving Word as a PDF or printing it as a standard PDF, print it as a PDF/X-1a:2001, which is designed for printer standards. To print this, select Adobe in your print menu. Then, click on properties, and change the standard default setting to PDF/X-1a:2001 format. This type of PDF will embed the fonts -- or if you have special fonts that can't be embedded, choose a more common font that can be. Then, upload that PDF to IngramSpark. For the cover, use the design created in CreateSpace as a guide to create the cover in the IngramSpark template. It's easiest to do this in InDesign or create the cover in Photoshop and save the final image as a PDF. The advantage of having the CreateSpace cover is you already have a design which is a timesaver, and if you work with a book designer, it will cost you much less -- perhaps $50-$100 to set up the design in the template, rather than $300-1500 for designing your cover from scratch.

4. Publish on IngramSpark as an e-book, using the appropriate ISBN from Bowker or obtain it from Ingram Spark. For the interior, convert your Word document into an epub file through Calibre or other software -- or hire someone who does these conversions. You can use the front cover design created through CreateSpace as a guide to create your e-book cover. If you have already created a 300 dpi front cover for a CreateSpace template, use that. Otherwise, use PhotoShop or a graphics designer to create your final 300 dpi cover.

5. Publish on Draft2Digital, Smashwords, or other e-book platforms. With Draft2Digital you can use your original Word document. Smashword has special requirements for the size of the type and spacing. Once your document is ready, upload the interior files. For the cover, you can generally use the cover you have already created for other programs, though you may need to make some adjustments for the size of the image.

Getting an ISBN

For each version of the book you publish -- hardcover, paper, and e-book -- you need a different ISBN, though you can use the same ISBN for a paperback published on CreateSpace and on IngramSpark, unless you opt fora free ISBN from CreateSpace. Then, you need a separate ISBN for a paperback published with IngramSpark. If you are using your own ISBN, follow the prompts for setting up your book, and when asked, indicate that you are using your own ISBN.

Selling Your Book

With CreateSpace and Kindle, once you approve the final proof, your book immediately goes on sale; with IngramSpark you can schedule a publication date for the future. A future pub date can be advantage if you want to do a special book launch. If so, allow a month or two, or even three, to get all of your PR and marketing arrangements in place.

If you publish on multiple platforms, be sure your price is the same for each version of the print book and for both e-book versions.

CHAPTER 5: DECIDING TO CREATE AN AUDIOBOOK

Until a year ago, I used to think of an audio book as a kind of add-on to publishing a paperback, e-book, and possibly a hardback. It seemed like one additional platform to make one's books as widely available as possible. But then, without my doing any promotion, I found my audio books were selling even more copies than my books on other platforms. I sold about 800 copies in 8 months, an average of 3 or 4 books a day, while one of my audiobooks sold nearly 200 copies. So why were these books doing so well compared to print sales?

By comparison, these numbers aren't very much, when some authors are doing extensive promotions and selling thousands of books a day. But when the average print or e-book is selling about 150 to 200 copies a year, audiobooks have become a growing market that can outperform other formats.

Why Are Audiobooks Growing So Rapidly

A key reason that audiobooks are doing so well now is because people are tending to read less and get their information in other ways, including on video and audio channels. Many people now listen to audio in their cars or on various playback devices when commuting by train or bus, and that can include listening to audiobooks, along with radio, audio files, CDs, and DVDs. So for an on-the-go audience, especially for millennials, now age 18 to 34 and about 75 million strong in the U.S., the audio format has become especially popular.

Another reason for the success of audiobooks is they are typically cheaper. They cost about $3.95 for a short book under 50 pages up to about $6.95 for a longer book of 400 to 500 pages.

Creating an Audiobook

Thus, creating an audiobook is increasingly the way to go. While you can create an audiobook as a stand-alone and publish it by itself, a good approach is to start with a print book or e-book and turn that text into the narration for an audiobook.

Certainly, you can create your audiobook by just reading it into a mike or your computer audio. But unless you know what you are doing to create a high-quality audio narration, some audiobook distributors will reject your book for not being professional enough.

Thus, either learn how to do a professional recording yourself, which involves getting some high quality audio recording equipment, including a professional mike, such as sold by Yeti. You also need to have a quiet setting, where you don't have extraneous sounds, or you need the equipment to filter out such background noise.

Hiring a Narrator

A good alternative to doing it yourself is to hire a skilled narrator. You can find freelance narrators on Audible.com (http://www.audible.com/int/Featured_Narrators), which sells audiobooks. Or do a search for audiobook narrators on Google. Still another source of narrators is through ACX (http://www.acx.com), which is owned by Amazon. You create an account, post that your book is open to auditions, and invite a narrator to narrate your book. You can either hire a narrator or propose a royalty split and an exclusive arrangement with ACX.

If you hire a narrator, figure on spending about $100 to $500 per finished hour, depending on the narrator's experience, with most averaging around $200 per finished hour. My own preference has been to find a volunteer narrator and split the royalty, and I have found narrators for all but two of my 65 audiobooks that I published so far through ACX. I have heard from voice-over professionals that the most skilled, professional narrators won't take a shared royalty gig, because the earnings typically aren't that much, but I have found some great narrators willing to take a chance on my books.

Generally, figure on the narrator taking two to three weeks for a short book of up to about 50 to 60 pages; about four to six weeks for a longer book of 100 pages or more. On average, the narrator will speak about 8500-9300 words a minute, so if you have a 50 page book with about 10,000 words, that'll be about an hour long. However, it commonly takes the narrator about two to three hours for each finished hour, because they have to take care of various technical details, such as editing, adjusting sound levels, and filtering out background noise.

CHAPTER 6: HIRING A NARRATOR THROUGH THE ACX PLATFORM

The ACX platform makes it easy to find a narrator, since they have hundreds of narrators in the system. You can either post a query about the availability of your book for narrators to audition to narrate your book or you can query particular narrators if you know them by name.

The service has a formal system which I have found works very well after using it to publish 65 books. To start, you set up your account by putting in some basic information about yourself, your contact information, and your bank and tax account. You can arrange for notifications about any activity in your account to be sent to your email, or you can see what's happening by going to your account.

Setting Up Your Book to Find a Narrator

In order to use the platform, you have to have a print or e-book already published on Amazon. You add your book by finding it on Amazon and indicating that "This is my book." Then, you create an offer for the narrator. There are two types of offers:

- If you want to hire a narrator, you will have a non-exclusive arrangement with ACX, get a 25% royalty, and you will own the book. Or you can agree to an exclusive agreement with ACX and you will get a 40% royalty.

- If you want a shared royalty arrangement, you agree to an exclusive with ACX and get a 40% royalty which you share with the narrator. You still have a copyright in the original book and audiobook, but you can't find another narrator and market the audiobook somewhere else.

You next have to provide some information about your book, including a short description, length of the book, and the type of narrator you are looking for. For example, indicate if you want a male or female narrator or both, want a narrator with a general American or other type of accent, or want an adult or younger narrator. You also indicate if you want to hire a narrator or propose a shared royalty arrangement.

You additionally create an audition file -- typically a file with 500-1500 words -- and upload that. Then, the prospective narrator creates and posts an audition recording, so you can listen to each narrator. After that, you can select the narrator you prefer and send an offer to narrate your book for a certain pay or royalty share. Usually you give the narrator 48 hours to respond, though you can make it 24 hours or offer a longer time frame.

Generally, I have gotten one to four narrators interested in reading my book, and on average, two to choose from. Probably you will get more auditions if you offer to hire a narrator, since there are many narrators, including some of the most experienced ones, who won't narrate a book on a shared royalty basis.

When you post your offer, you also indicate when you expect the narrator to complete the first 15 minutes, and the whole project, clicking on a calendar to indicate this. After that, your offer remains open until a narrator accepts your offer, though you can remove it or repost it later if you haven't gotten any interest in your offer, or perhaps you might want to change this from a royalty share to a work-for-hire arrangement.

From a Narrator Accepting Your Offer to a Completed Audiobook

Once a narrator accepts your offer, you have to send the whole manuscript in a PDF or .doc(x) file. If there are photos or illustrations, you generally will provide these in a separate PDF which the ACX staff can set up with a link for the customer to download, and the staff will post instructions for the customer to do this. Additionally, the narrator will mention in the beginning of the narration that this PDF is available. If the book has only a few unimportant photos, you don't have to include them in the audiobook, and the narrator will read the text as if the photos aren't there.

For the next step, the narrator will send you first 15 minutes, after which you can approve the narration or ask for changes. For example, you might suggest the narrator should read your book with more passion and enthusiasm or should tone down an overly emotional reading, which I have done in a couple of cases. Or if a narrator isn't pronouncing something correctly or is reading the text too fast or slowly, you can recommend what the narrator should do, which is again something I have done. Then, the narrator will make any corrections and send you another 15 minutes to review.

In the meantime, you can post the final cover art, which has to be in a square format of at least 2400x2400 pixels. Since your front cover is normally in a 6"x9", 7"x10", 8"x10" or other book size format, you can't use it as is. However, if you have a white or black background, sometimes you can increase the canvas size to create a square. Or it may be possible to use Photoshop or other graphics editing programs crop the cover and move your name as the author or the title around on the original cover design. Otherwise, you have to rework the cover to fit this square format. You need to have this completed cover ready, when you provide your final approval for the book.

After you approve the first 15 minutes, the narrator will complete the whole book, and can post the audio files as he or she goes along for you to review. Or you can wait until all the files are up and you get an announcement from ACX that the full manuscript is ready for your review. Again you can make any suggestions for changes or approve the whole thing.

You can make a careful review of the whole narration if you want, although my approach has been to spot check the beginnings of a sampling of files. Then, if all sounds okay, I'll approve the book and let the ACX reviewers listen to everything, since they are skilled at noticing any errors, and especially any audio problems that the narrator has to fix. For instance, in one case, a narrator had a lot of background noise and didn't know how to correct this, until I put her in touch with someone with the necessary filter equipment, which saved the book. Otherwise, I would have had to start again by finding another narrator.

In most cases, I have found that narrators make the agreed upon deadlines, though some will ask for a few extra weeks because something unexpected has happened in their life, and normally I agree. ACX is also fairly lax about holding narrators to strict standards, as long as the author is onboard. However, if the delay is much too long or the narrator says that he or she can't complete the project, you can explain this to the ACX staff. If the narrator acknowledges and agrees to this, ACX will dissolve the contract and you can look for another narrator. So far, that happened to me just once, and I quickly found a new narrator.

In general, I have found that narrators more quicly volunteer for a royalty arrangement with a short book, because they can complete it more quickly -- in just a few hours. In fact, the two books where I wasn't able to find a narrator were much longer books – one was a nonfiction book about ethics that clocked in at about 400 pages; the other was a suspense thriller that was about 350 pages long. Also, most delays have occurred with longer books. By contrast, some of the narrators I worked with finished the much shorter books of about 3000-5000 words or less in a few days.

Commonly, the entire narration arrangement can go back and forth on the ACX platform without any direct communication with the narrator, although I have usually given the narrator accepting my offer my phone number, if the narrator wants to call with any questions. You can also send the narrator your direct email, and I have sometimes done so for more extended communication. Otherwise, using the ACX platform to communicate with the narrator works fine.

Once you send your final approval, you should send any PDF with photos or illustrations directly to the support staff at ACX, along with a note that this is to accompany a particular manuscript. Plus your cover art should be completed and uploaded at this point.

Then, it typically takes about 10 days for a final approval. After that your audiobook will soon be available on Audible, Amazon, and iTunes.

If there is a problem -- usually some audio glitch that has to be fixed, ACX will let you know and also advise the narrator to make the requested fix. Some typical complaints are that there is background noise, the audio track lacks the necessary 30 seconds or so of space before the narration starts, or there are mic clicks on the narration. Once the narrator makes any requested fixes, the ACX staff will review the project again. Or if the narrator can't fix the audio as previously noted, ACX will dissolve your contract with the narrator, and you can start again.

Assuming that the audiobook is completed successfully, you'll get a note that it has been approved. Then, you will find it on sale on Audible, Amazon, and iTunes in about a week to 10 days. Plus you may also get 20 or so coupons you can give out for free promotional listens to your book -- or at least I got these when I first started creating audio books.

So now your audiobook is done, and it will be priced automatically based on its length from $3.95 to about $6.95. Then, ACX will give you a royalty statement of your earnings each month. If you want to chart your progress more regularly, you will find the number of sales updated every day or two in your account on the ACX website. You'll see a bright orange number and below it a link to your sales dashboard, where you can see how each audiobook you have created is doing. After that, about the 20th of each month, you'll get a royalty statement, and about a week later, you'll see the money magically appear in your bank account.

To increase your sales even more, you can promote your audiobook or combine any promotion for your print or e-book with an audiobook promotion, giving potential buyers even more choice on what to buy.

CHAPTER 7: THE BASICS OF CREATING YOUR BOOK AS A COURSE

Another format that is growing in popularity is the online course, which can also be turned into an interactive online or face-to-face workshop. Often a nonfiction book is the basis for such a course. So consider the course as one more format for your book -- and just as an audiobook can often sell more than a print book, so can a course. In fact, if your book is on a popular topic, you may be able to develop that into a top course generating thousands of dollars in income each day.

I didn't realize the power of courses until I started taking a series of courses on online and email marketing. Soon I began getting ads on Facebooks for courses on creating email lists and selling e-books, followed by ads for creating and marketing courses. Now there are even platforms for selling online courses or making them available to subscribers, such as Thrive Courses (https://thrivecourses.com), which was developed by the workshop leader of a Meetup group and Mastermind group I am part of.

Additionally, there are now multiple platforms for anyone seeking to create a course, which meets some basic criteria, such as Teachable (www.teachable.com), which specializes in online courses, and ClickBank (www.clickbank.com), the biggest online platform for selling just about anything that can be sold online.

Of course, you can teach a course without a book or create a course you later turn into a book. But you can also turn a book into a course -- and you can use your course to sell your print, e-book, and audiobook, as well as other products. Or someone can simply take your course.

What Makes a Good Course

Most commonly, popular online courses are all about teaching someone how to do something -- particularly how to make money, save money, improve relationships, gain more success in work or business, become healthier, lose weight, or master a skill or hobby. As a result, the most popular genres for courses are love, money, relationships, health, happiness, and success. Plus, some top selling courses are targeted to achieving success in a particular industry, such as on how to write, publish, and market books, write scripts, make films, or start a business.

So if you've written a novel, a course based on it might not work, but a course on how to write a novel or on how to turn your book into a best seller might be a success, such as proven by Nick Stephenson, a successful mystery writer, who wrote a course on how to get your first ten thousand (10k) readers (https://www.yourfirst10kreaders.com).

To determine if you've got a good idea for a course, research what niches are popular and what course are already offered in a niche, just as you might research the competition and market for a print or e-book. Generally, you will find an overabundance of courses once a niche becomes popular, just as certain niches have become very popular in print, e-books, and audiobooks, such as the self-help, popular business, relationships, and diet and health books. Thus, do some research on what other courses are in your area. You want to create something that's new and different, and then market and promote it, much like you would a book. One good way to do this research is to put "courses" and the topic you want your course to be about in a Google search.

In naming your course, you might use the title of your book as your course title, if it is short and to the point. Alternatively, you can come up with a catchy title for your course and indicate that it is based on your book. Or use your subtitle for the course title, if it makes it clearer how this subject will help the person who takes the course.

Creating Your Course

Once you decide on the subject of your course, whether it is based on your print book or not, the next step is to structure your course so it contains a series of modules and classes within each module.

Commonly, structure your course with an introduction describing what the course is about, what the person will learn, and how the course is set up. Then, turn your subject matter into a series of modules that are like chapters in a book. Generally, each module will include a series of two to five videos of about 3-10 minutes, though some can be as long as 20-25 minutes. Plus each module or the classes in it commonly include links, so the viewer can download some or all of the following:

- a video, audio track, or PowerPoint of the slides used in the video,
- a cheat sheet with highlights of the course,
- a PDF with the contents of the video and sometimes a more complete discussion of the topics covered in the video.

Most courses also have a menu on the side or on top with a drop-down menu that lists all of the modules in the course, so a viewer can easily find the different modules and classes in it. Often each module will include a section to indicate that one has completed a particular class or module, which will show as a checkmark or color for each completed course. Additionally, you will often see an arrow pointing to the next class or module in the series, once you finish each class or all the classes in a module.

CHAPTER 8: ORGANZING YOUR COURSE AND CREATING YOUR VIDEOS AND OTHER MATERIALS

Now that you understand the basics for creating a course, here are more detailed guidelines on how to structure it, create videos for it, and price it.

Organizing Your Course

Create an introduction for your course – preferably as a video – as well as introductions for each module or classes in that module. Then, create a video for your course materials, along with any supplementary materials, for each class, such as PDFs and/or

PowerPoints. Combine a series of classes into modules, and then that's your course.

A good way to organize all of your videos and supplementary materials into an overall course structure is to include two to five classes in a module, which might be comparable to the parts of a book. For example, Module 1 is based on Part I of your book, Module 2 is based on Part II, and so forth.

However, while its ideal for your course structure to parallel the organization of your book, this doesn't always work, such as if your book is not divided into parts or has only two or three parts. In that case, divide up the whole book into modules, or divide up the chapters in each part to create additional modules.

You can either divide the modules up into classes or list all of the classes and group them into modules. However you do this, give the module a name that reflects the classes in it, and name the classes, as well. If the classes or modules are based directly on chapters and sections in your book, use those names; otherwise, create short, compelling titles for your modules and classes.

For example, Nick Stephenson's course on Your First 10K Readers, with 59 classes, ranging from about 15-30 minutes each, is structured like this:

- Introduction: Start Here
- Your Core Training: 6 Modules
   - Module 1- Rule the Retailers
   - Module 2 - Drive Endless Traffic
   - Module 3 - Convert Traffic into Subscribers
   - Module 4 - Engage Your Audience
   - Module 5 - The Ultimate Launch
   - Module 6 - Facebook: Profit on Autopilot

Each module lists several classes. Half have four classes; the others have three, five, or six classes, and the length of each class is listed. For example, in Module one, the classes are:

Video 1: Rule the Retailers: 31 minutes
Video 2: Merchandising: 23 minutes
Video 3: Exclusivity vs. Broad Reach: 20 minutes
Video 4: Pricing: 24 minutes

Plus Stephenson includes several additional modules for advanced training based on about 35 to 75minute interviews with 6 writers, tools of the trade, swipe files of email exchanges, 5 coaching calls, and links to a Facebook group with a community of writers, where you can ask questions about implementing the training. Thus, this is a very comprehensive training program that is very well thought out and organized, and it provides a good model to follow in designing your own course.

While Stephenson's videos are longer than most of the videos for the email marketing classes I participated in -- usually they were about 7-15 minutes – his course structure illustrates how a course is put together.

You can make your own course shorter or longer, depending on how much you have to say on your topic, although these courses generally have at least 6 or 7 classes. Once you have about 9 or more classes, you can divide them into at least three modules with at least three classes in each module. Otherwise, with less than 8 or 9 classes, set up your course with a series of classes. If you have the material, you can add interviews, coaching calls, blogs, other bonuses, and links to a Facebook group.

If you have advanced trainings or products or services to sell, you can include them in your course guide menu, too, such as by listing "Advanced Courses" or "Products Available."

Creating Videos for Your Course

Think of these videos as the heart of your online course. So you have to make them compelling and engaging, mostly by using PowerPoints with voice-overs that sometimes include graphics, video clips, and cutaways to online interviews and websites.

Usually viewers want to see who you are, so ideally include a short video introducing yourself to viewers. This introduction can be at the beginning of the course or in a separate introductory video. Once you have introduced yourself in the first video, in future videos you can simply say something like "Hi, again. This is…" Then, your introduction can briefly note what viewers will learn in the video, refer back to what you have taught in a previous video if there was one, and state how important or useful this information will be.

For example, Nick Stephenson begins the video for each class with about 15-30 seconds to say hello, recap what everyone learned in the last video, and note what everyone will now learn. Next, he makes a comment like: "So now let's get to it." Then, the video for the class, consisting of a series of PowerPoint slides and voiceovers, begins.

If you are doing a direct to camera approach, where you talk directly to the viewer, include cutaways to slides, images, charts, a bulletin board, or graphics, so your video is not just a talking head. Another approach that some course presenters use is to feature themselves talking in a small box on the top of the screen, usually on the top right, which remains there while the presentation continues in the main video screen.

Or commonly, and for most of the videos I have seen, the course consists of a series of PowerPoint slides with a voice-over, along with many cutaways to illustrate what the presenter is talking about. Additionally, below the video are links to download the video, audio, PDF, and other materials.

For cutaways, you can include photos, video clips, graphic images, illustrations, cartoons, charts, graphs, much like you might think of adding images to a book, plus video clips to an e-book. Manipulating all of these events is a little like being a movie producer, such as Ken Burns, who has created a series of historical documentaries, using photos from the archives.

Don't have the time, interest, or ability in doing all this yourself? You can hire professionals who will put these courses together for you, or you can readily do much of this course creation yourself. For example, use Facebook Live or an SLR camera on a tripod to record yourself speaking. Use some software and services to help you put these PowerPoint presentations and cutaways together, such as Animoto (www.animoto.com) or

VideoBuilder (http://www.videobuilder.io), where you upload your slides, photos, video clips, and other elements together to make a short intro or promotional video. .

For longer videos, you can organize your PowerPoint slides and clips and add your voice over, using video editing software from Camtasia (https://www.techsmith.com/video-editor.html), or you can add Camtasia as a video enhancer on PowerPoint 10 and above. Just go to "Add-Ins" and add Camtasia. The way this program works is that you speak as you move from slide to slide. You say whatever you want to say for each slide, then click to go to the next slide, and speak some more. When you get to the end of the slide show, you indicate you are finished. Thereafter, you can save that PowerPoint as an mp4 video and add that to your course.

Pricing Your Course

One of the most sensitive and important considerations is how to price your course. In general, if this is an introductory, stand-alone course with a small number of classes, say 10 classes or less, you can price it at the low end as a single purchase of about $27 to $47. If your course is a little longer – say 11 - 20 classes, price it for a little more – say $97 to $147. Even longer – say 21-35 classes – price it for $197 to $297. Or if you have a more advanced, specialized course, start off with a higher pricing structure, such as starting at $147 to $247, and charge $499 to $599 of more for future programs.

For the most advanced, developed courses, such as one with 50 or 60 classes, like Nick Stephenson created, you can charge even more -- from about $597 to $997 are common amounts. But once you charge, offer a payment plan, such as $49 or $97 a month, so the viewer can pay a small amount now to get started, though the full price will typically be about 10-20% more when they finally pay in full.

Once you set the basic price, you can consider different pricing specials, which is common in the online course industry, such as a super low price to buy now (ie: pay $27 for a course valued at $97; $97 for a course valued at $497; $147 for a course valued at $997, and so on. Or buy it now before the price goes up, based on a price increase in increments with each purchase, such as an increase of $1, $5, or $10 with each additional purchase, or the price can be set to go up automatically by $1 to $5 every hour or two. Since pricing involves all kinds of marketing considerations about what to charge, when, how to use discounts and coupons, joint promotions, and more, I'll discuss this at length in another series of articles or books on marketing and sales techniques.

So now you're ready to start creating your course. Meanwhile, as you decide how to structure it and develop your materials, the next step is to start promoting your course to get sign-ups, and I'll cover that in a future article series or book.

CHAPTER 9: CREATING YOUR BOOK OR CHAPTERS AS A PDF

Still another way to format your book is as a PDF, which you can create, promote and sell in various ways. Here are some of them:
 - Create individual chapters as blogs, which you can use to build traffic to your website.
 - Using a chapter or section of a chapter as a "gift" to offer to prospects in a sales funnel. The idea is they like this material so much that they go on to purchase your whole book or related services and product.
 - Use the PDF as a bonus for people who buy your book or take a course from you.
 - Write individual chapters as articles or blogs, which you later combine into a complete book;

- Use the PDF as a handout in a workshop or introductory meeting about what you do;

- Sell a short PDF on a specialized topic, where you are offering high-value information, such as new investment opportunities, how to save money on getting a mortgage, or how recently passed laws will affect one's business. Such high-value information can be produced on even one or two pages, since individuals are buying the information and are not concerned that this PDF is much shorter than a book.

Typically, PDF books range from a few pages to about 35 to 50 pages, and often they are double-spaced like a manuscript rather than a published book. Sometimes they are straight text, but often they include photos, illustrations, graphs, and charts.

Such a short PDF can also be published as a very short book, such as through CreateSpace or IngramSpark, but it doesn't have to be. Rather, you can offer the PDF for free, as an incentive or bonus or for sale. In either case, you provide it in the form of a file to download. You can send this link manually, if you have a small number of requests or orders, or you can set it up with one of the automatic responders, such as AWeber (www.aweber.com), GetResponse (www.getresponse.com), or MailChimp (www.mailchimp.com), so anytime someone places an order or send an email in response to an ad, they automatically get a link to your PDF which they can download.

Creating Your PDF

Since virtually everyone knows how to create and read a PDF from Adobe, I won't describe how to do that. But what many people don't know is how to create a printer-friendly high resolution PDF with embedded fonts. You need this type of PDF for some printer programs, such as IngramSpark, which I already described. Plus you may want a high-resolution file if you are selling your PDFs direct, especially if you are including photos, illustrations, and charts, which will show off better in a higher resolution PDF.

The way to create a high-resolution PDF is to print your original Word document as a PDF, rather than using the "Save as PDF" function. Or in an Apple MacIntosh environment, you can do the equivalent in Pages or save your document as a Word file.

When you print your Word or other document, indicate that you want to print an Adobe PDF and go to "Properties." Then, instead of using the standard default setting, indicate that you want to print the document as a PDF/X-1a:2001. That setting will provide the higher resolution and embed any fonts. If you have used fonts you can't embed, such as special fonts requiring a license to use them, you will get a message accordingly that the fonts can't be embedded. Then, select another more common font that will embed.

Creating a Cover for Your PDF

While you don't have to create a cover for your PDF, this is a nice touch. You simply place this cover as the first page of your PDF, and you can easily insert this page after you complete the rest of the document. You can also use the cover to promote your PDF on your website or other online sales network, such as ClickBank (www.clickbank.com).

To create the cover, create a design as you would for the front cover of a printed book or e-book. You can use illustrations or stock photos, or have a designer create your cover, whatever you want. Just design it with the view that you will be using the cover as a promotional tool for selling your book from your website or landing page.

Including Sales Material in Your Book

You can include a sales page, just as you would in a print-book or e-book, in the front of the PDF, in the back, or both. You can use this page to sell your other books or whatever you want -- from other PDFs or published books for sale to related products and services.

The sales page should include a link to your website or landing page where people can obtain your published books or learn about other products and services. This sales page can also include links to Amazon, if you have any books or products for sale there, since you won't have any problems for pitching a competing sales platform, as is the case if you publish an e-book on IngramSpark and include a link to a book sold on Amazon, since Apple, which is one of IngramSpark's distributors, won't market a book with an Amazon link. But you aren't selling your PDF through any of these distributors and retailers. Rather, you are selling it direct to customers through your website or landing page, or through an email or online marketing campaign.

Selling Your Book through Your Website, Landing Page, or Online Marketing

Deciding exactly how to best market and promote your PDF is a marketing question on how to best reach your audience. So I will leave that for a future book. Here I just want to cover the basics of how to sell or use your PDF as a gift or incentive. The four basic methods which you can use individually or combine in various ways are the following:

- Create an offer on your website. To do this, create a section on your home page or on a sales page, where you feature the cover of your book and the text of your offer. If a person clicks to know more or purchase what you are offering, you can then obtain information from them. A typical sequence is to either have them purchase the item if it is for sale with a credit card or PayPal account or to send them to a landing page to access the gift or incentive. There you ask for their email and send an email to them, which includes the link to click to get their PDF. The reason for the extra step of asking for their email and sending the link to the free gift there is to verify that they have given you a valid email.

- <u>Create an offer on a landing page</u>. This works the same way as an offer on your website, except you normally have a stand-alone page that describes your PDF and provides a button to click to buy or a button to provide their email, so you can send them the gift or incentive.

- <u>Offer your PDF as a gift in an email campaign</u>. In this case, your offer comes from an email sent to a prospective customer or client. Then, anyone interested in learning more can click a button to go to your website or landing page, and then you proceed above.

- <u>Offer your PDF as a gift in an ad campaign</u>. In this case, your offer comes from an ad, such as through Facebook or Google AdWords. As with the email campaign, the ad should direct the person to your website or landing page, where you provide more detail about the offer, and then you proceed as above.

Turning Your PDF into a Published Book

Just as you can turn a series of articles or blogs into a published book, so too can you turn a PDF or series of PDF into a book published in any of the other formats. For example, you can create additional chapters to build on a chapter turned into a PDF to complete the whole book. Or if you have turned a blog or article into a PDF, you can combine a series of them into a book.

Once you have created enough short PDFs, you can combine the PDFs and publish them in any of the formats previously described -- print, e-books, audiobooks, or a class in a course.

One advantage of starting out by distributing a PDF is this can be a quick way to get started towards the larger project. The PDF can also be a way to test the waters to see what kind of interest there is in the subject. And the PDF can be a way to introduce yourself and your ideas for a larger project to an audience interested in this subject, such as when you are setting up an introductory Facebook group or face-to-face meeting.

So if you aren't already publishing a book, a PDF to determine if there is interest in a paid workshop on the topic can be a good way to get started. Or use your PDF as a supplement, or loss leader gift to help introduce and promote your published book.

ABOUT THE AUTHOR

GINI GRAHAM SCOTT, Ph.D., J.D., is a nationally known writer, consultant, speaker, and seminar leader, specializing in business and work relationships, professional and personal development, social trends, and popular culture. She has published over 50 books with major publishers. She has worked with dozens of clients on memoirs, self-help, popular business books, and film scripts. Writing samples are at www.ginigrahamscott.com and www.changemakerspublishingandwriting.com. She is a Huffington Post regular columnist, commenting on social trends, business, and everyday life at www.huffingtonpost.com/gini-graham-scott.

She is the founder of Changemakers Publishing, featuring books on work, business, psychology, social trends, and self-help. It has published over 100 print, e-books, and audiobooks. She has licensed several dozen books for foreign sales, including the UK, Russia, Korea, Spain, and Japan.

She has received national media exposure for her books, including appearances on *Good Morning America, Oprah,* and *CNN.* She has been the producer and host of a talk show series, *Changemakers*, featuring interviews on social trends.

Her books on business relationships and professional development include:

Self-Publishing Secrets (Changemakers Publishing)
Turn Your Dreams into Reality (Llewellyn)
Resolving Conflict (Changemakers Publishing)
A Survival Guide for Working with Bad Bosses (AMACOM)
A Survival Guide for Working with Humans (AMACOM)
Credit Card Fraud with Jen Grondahl Lee (Rowman)
Lies and Liars: How and Why Sociopaths Lie (Skyhorse Publishing)

Scott is also active in a number of community and business groups, including the Lafayette, Pleasant Hill, and Danville Chambers of Commerce. She is a graduate of the prestigious Leadership Contra Costa program, is a7 member of two B2B groups in Danville and Walnut Creek, and a BNI member. She is the organizer of six Meetup groups in the film and publishing industries with over 6000 members in Los Angeles and the San Francisco Bay Area. She does workshops and seminars on the topics of her books.

She received her Ph.D. from the University of California, Berkeley, and her J.D. from the University of San Francisco Law School. She has received several MAs at Cal State University, East Bay.

CHANGEMAKERS PUBLISHING
3527 Mt. Diablo Blvd., #273
Lafayette, CA 94549
changemakers@pacbell.net . (925) 385-0608
www.changemakerspublishingandwriting.com

www.ingramcontent.com/pod-product-compliance
Lightning Source LLC
Chambersburg PA
CBHW071544080526
44588CB00011B/1784